FANTASTIC FACES

FANTASTIC FACES

by SNAZAROO

Kingfisher

NEW YORK

Editor: Jacqui Bailey
Face Painting: Lauren Cornell, Jenny Cornell,
Rebecca Kew, Florencia Sittoni, Tina Hodgkiss,
James Pena-Romero, Lyn Muscroft, Sharon Davenport,
Wilhelmina Barnden
Design: Pinpoint Design Co.
Photography: Roger Crump
Cover Design: Terry Woodley

With special thanks to all the children and
their parents who helped us to make this book.

KINGFISHER
Larousse Kingfisher Chambers Inc.
95 Madison Avenue
New York, New York 10016

First American edition 1994
10 9 8 7 6 5 4 3 2 1

LIBRARY OF CONGRESS CATALOGING-IN-PUBLICATION DATA
Snazaroo.
    Fantastic faces / by Snazaroo.—1st American ed.
        p. cm.
    1. Face painting—Juvenile literature. [1. Face painting.]
I. Title.
TT911.S63 1995
745.5—dc20 94-3425 CIP AC

ISBN 1-85697-540-1

Printed in Spain

CONTENTS

About This Book   8

Materials   10

1 SIMPLE AND QUICK   **12**
Clowns   14
Spots and Stripes   16
Crazy Animals   18

2 TAKING A LITTLE LONGER   **20**
Party Time   22
Fur and Feathers   24
Carnival   26
Rough and Tumble   28

3 BODY PAINTING AND MOTIFS   **30**
Beautiful Bodies   32
Magic Motifs   34

4 PUTTING YOUR SKILLS TO WORK   **36**
Simple Special Effects   38
Dancers   40
Characters   41
Running a Workshop   46

ABOUT THIS BOOK

All children love to dress up and play make-believe, whether they are doing it just for fun at home or for a special event. Face paints add the final touch to any costume. In fact, face paints are often all you need to create a whole fantasy world of characters.

Fantastic Faces is all about the fantastic effects that can be achieved using a particular type of face paint made from water-based makeup. This type of makeup was originally developed for the theater, but it is increasingly being used for other purposes as more and more people discover how easy it is to apply.

Getting Started

Face painting has been growing in popularity, becoming an attraction at children's parties, charity events, and carnivals. With the type of water-based makeup now available, really startling effects and designs can be achieved with a little practice and a steady hand. In this book you will find a selection of face-painting designs, ranging from the very quick and simple to those that need a little more care and thought.

If you have never done any face painting before, you will find a full description of basic techniques on page 12, along with a simple step-by-step explanation of how the paint is applied. After that, just copy the face designs in the book, follow the stages described, and you will be amazed to find how easy it is. Start with the faces in the "Simple and Quick" section first, then go on to the slightly more complicated faces shown in the section called "Taking a Little Longer."

A Last Word

As a face painter you will probably find yourself in great demand at schools, nursery schools, clubs, or any other place where young people gather. Why not run a workshop and pass your skills on? On the last page we give you some suggestions on how to get started. Workshops can be great fun for everyone, and you may even pick up some ideas for new faces.

Moving On

Once you are comfortable with the techniques, you will find that there are all sorts of things you can do, including body painting and simple theatrical makeup for school plays and amateur productions. In the section called "Putting Your Skills to Work" you will find some simple special-effects techniques for adding a false beard or mustache, changing the shape of a nose or chin, or even making someone look older than they really are.

All of these techniques can be used to enhance character faces for stage plays or simply for a fantastic masquerade costume. We have also included examples of several of the most popular characters that pop up all the time in amateur plays, along with some ideas for making the costumes.

9

MATERIALS

Face painters usually build up a fairly wide collection of materials for their makeup kits. This can be done gradually, but you will need a few essential items before you start painting.

Most makeup artists treat themselves to a case with a handle: something that is easily transportable. An ordinary plastic toolbox is a good solution—these are available from most hardware stores and usually contain several sections to keep your makeup in.

The Makeup

Water-based makeup has been around for many years, but was often thought of as inferior to the greasepaint used by the theater world. Now it has been discovered by face painters because it is easier and more practical to use on children.

Water-based makeup is applied quickly and easily. It can be put on with a sponge for a base color and a brush for fine lines and details. It can also be used on the body and can be applied to the hair with a sponge or a dry toothbrush.

Colors can be mixed for a greater variety of shades, and water-based makeup dries very fast and will not smudge—so long as you don't get it wet. Best of all, it washes off with just water and a little soap and can be washed out of most types of clothing.

Water-based makeup can be bought in paint palettes containing a selection of colors or in individual handy-sized jars. At present, it is still most widely available through stores selling theatrical products. The range of colors is quite varied and also includes fluorescent colors.

A twelve-color palette is sufficient for a beginner to start with and will enable you to copy most of the faces in this book, but if you want to do a lot of painting you may find the jars more economical.

Brushes and Sponges

Makeup sponges are the best type to use. Sponges designed for use with water-based makeup are made of soft foam and give a good base color. You can also buy sponges cut into wedges, which give you both a broad surface and a fine edge. A stipple sponge is useful for creating a stubble effect on chins and for applying aging techniques and special effects, such as bruises and scrapes. A theatrical supplier will have a wide range of sponges, but if there is no supplier in your area, you can use the foam latex sponges available from most drugstores.

It is a good idea to have a fairly wide selection of different-sized makeup brushes. We use sable or imitation sable makeup brushes. The latter are the best type of brush for face painting, as they give more control. They are made from synthetic fibers and are therefore much less expensive than real sable brushes.

Glitter

Glitter makeup can work beautifully on some face designs, but make sure that you use glitter gel—never the dry glitter that is intended for gluing on paper. Glitter gel can be bought in a range of colors in small tubes and jars. Do not put glitter makeup too close to the eyes, and do not use it on small children as they might rub it into their eyes.

Special Effects

There are two very basic special-effects materials which can be used in a variety of ways—these are modeling wax and crepe hair.

Modeling wax is a firm wax that is used for changing the shape of some parts of the face, such as the nose, forehead, and chin. It is also used for making scars and wounds.

Crepe hair is used for making beards and mustaches. It is bought by the length in the form of a braid and is glued to the skin using water soluble spirit gum.

Another material you may find useful is tooth black for blacking out front teeth. This comes in a small bottle and looks like black nail polish. To use it, first dry the teeth with a tissue and then paint it on. It can be brushed off with a toothbrush and toothpaste.

All of these special-effects products are suitable for use with children. However, do check with your supplier first, as there is a large range of products to choose from.

Finally, always make sure that you carry a clean container for water to clean your brushes and sponges; plenty of tissues or pre-moistened tissues for cleaning off dirty faces before you start; a bright-colored towel for laying out your paints and brushes on; and a mirror.

Most of these materials should be obtainable from any good theatrical supplier.

1 SIMPLE AND QUICK

Basic Techniques

Water-based makeup is very easy to apply. Once you have mastered the basic techniques described here and have had time to practice, you will find that you will be able to produce faces that look very professional.

1. Always check that your model does not suffer from any skin disorder. Water-based makeup has been highly tested and is completely non-toxic, but if you are in any doubt, it is a good idea to test a little makeup on the inside of the wrist to see if any irritation occurs.

2. Always keep your materials (including jars, brushes, and towels) scrupulously clean, and change the water regularly.

3. Water-based makeup should be applied directly to a clean, dry skin. There is no need to use a moisturizer first.

4. When face painting, it is best if you stand up and your model sits on a high stool. Keep your model steady by resting one hand on his or her head.

5. Always apply the base color first with a sponge that is barely damp. If the sponge is too wet your base will become streaky. Some colors make better bases than others, so try to experiment with them. For a deeper color, allow the first coat to dry and then apply a second coat.

6. When you are using a brush to paint in the details, try to put on the light colors first, and use good bold strokes.

7. When face painting children, keep designs simple and quick. Children do not like to sit for longer than about five minutes. If you are doing the makeup for an amateur play and need more detailed faces, try to choose a model who will sit still for a longer period.

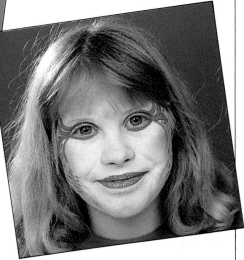

Step 1—Using a barely damp sponge, apply a white base.

Step 2—Using a barely damp sponge, blend in another color around the edge of the face, working your strokes outward.

Step 3—Using a brush and various other colors, decorate the eyes, lips, and cheeks.

8. Take care when painting around the eyes. Small children who have never had their face painted before may be nervous. When painting the top eyelids, ask your models to keep their eyes closed until the paint is dry. When painting along the bottom eye line, ask your model to look up as you do so. Do not take the paint too close to the eyes.

These space cadets are easy enough for any beginner to try. Here we have used metallic water makeup for the base and lots of bright fluorescent colors for the zigzags. Apply the base color first, with a barely damp sponge. Paint in the zig-zag shapes with a brush. Paint the mouth last.

13

Clowns

Clowns are good faces to begin with when you are first learning how to face paint. You can experiment with lots of different designs, using bold shapes and bright colors. Always start with a white base.

BOW TIE CLOWN:

1. Using a barely damp sponge, apply a white base over the whole face.

2. Use a brush to paint in blue above the eyes, and outline them in pink.

3. Using a brush, paint in the red nose and mouth.

4. Outline the eyes, nose, and mouth in black.

5. Paint in black triangles under the eyes.

6. Add highlights using a little white paint on the tip of the nose, and white and yellow on the cheeks.

VARIATIONS:

The two clowns shown on the right were painted in much the same way—the only difference being the colors used and the pattern of the shapes.

Practice with the faces shown on these pages first, then try inventing your own.

Spots and Stripes

STRIPES:

1. Use a large brush to paint in the blue, yellow, and pink stripes down the face.

2. Use a thinner brush to paint the two squiggly black lines over the borders.

With this face, the hair has been covered with a rubber skullcap, bought from a party store and then painted over with water-based makeup to match the design on the face.

SCHOOLGIRL:

1. Apply a yellow base with a damp sponge.

2. Using a brush, paint in blue eyeglasses.

3. Paint in different-colored spots.

4. Paint the lips in a matching color.

CARTOON CAT:

1. Apply a yellow base using a damp sponge.

2. Use a brush to paint in the pink eyelids, and outline in blue with a thin brush.

3. Using a brush, paint in the blue nose and mouth, the blue and pink zigzags, and pink whiskers.

JACK-O'-LANTERN:

1. Apply an orange base using a damp sponge.

2. Using a brush, paint in the white eyes and the teeth.

3. Paint in black outlines around the eyes and the mouth.

4. Use a thin brush to paint the thin black lines down the face.

DIZZY DOG:

1. Apply a thin white base using a sponge.

2. Blend in light brown around the outer part of the face using a sponge.

3. Using a brush, paint in light brown patches above the eyes and on the nose and cheeks.

4. Outline all of the patches in dark brown or black.

5. Paint in the red tongue, and outline it in black with a thin brush.

6. Using a brush, outline the eyes in black as shown, and paint in the black nose, mouth, and whiskers.

NAUGHTY MONKEY:

1. Using a sponge, apply a yellow base.

2. Using a brush, paint in the white eyes.

3. Using a large brush, paint in the shaped outline around the face, and fill in around it with dark brown color, taking the paint up to the hairline.

4. Using a brush, draw the outline of the mouth, then fill in with dark brown.

5. Using a brush, paint the black eyebrows and outline the eyes.

6. Paint in the black nose and the black lines over the mouth, and highlight the mouth in yellow and orange.

To make the monkey's ears, cut out two ear shapes from cardboard and cover them in brown fabric, or paint them. Cut two moon shapes from orange felt, and glue them onto the ears. Glue or sew the ears to a narrow headband.

2 TAKING A LITTLE LONGER

Now it's time to become a little more adventurous. The following designs look more difficult and will take you longer to do when you first try them, but with practice you will soon build up your speed and confidence.

Try to memorize some of these designs so that you can do them without looking at the pictures. This will save you time, and you will soon find that you can paint some of these faces in just five minutes.

UNDER THE SEA:

1. Using a damp sponge, apply a white base over the forehead.

2. Use a damp sponge to apply a blue base around the eyes and over the rest of the face.

3. Using a brush, paint in blue waves and lips.

4. Paint in the octopus, starfish, crab, and fish.

Try the same face using other ideas of your own, such as an anchor, a shipwreck, a treasure chest, or a seahorse. Sketch each one on a piece of paper first, until you are happy with both the shape and the color.

ON THE BEACH:

1. Apply yellow paint over the bottom half of the face, using a damp sponge.

2. Using a damp sponge, apply blue paint over the rest of the face.

3. Using the same sponge, blend a little white paint over the forehead to create a misty sky.

4. Using a brush, paint palm trees with dark brown trunks and leaves of two different shades of green.

5. Highlight the trees with a little white paint, using a fine brush.

6. With the same brush, paint in some dark blue and white waves across the cheeks.

7. Using a fine brush, paint in the black birds and the red starfish.

There are lots of other beach objects you could use in this design instead. For example, why not try deckchairs, ice-cream cones, buckets and shovels, seaweed, and sailboats?

BELLY DANCER:

1. Use ordinary pink blusher on the cheeks.

2. Using water-based makeup, paint in the blue eyes and eye decoration with a brush.

3. Paint in gold eyes and eye decoration.

4. Paint the gold chain using a thin brush, and then the blue diamond shape.

5. Use water-soluble spirit gum to stick on the sequins and the star.

6. Paint on red lips and add gold glitter gel.

BUTTERFLY:

1. Apply a white base with a sponge.

2. Use a sponge to blend in pink and yellow around the outer edge of the face.

3. Use a thin brush to paint the butterfly shape in lilac, and fill in with pastel colors.

4. Paint in the pink nose and red lips.

5. Paint the black antennae with a thin brush.

6. Decorate with pink glitter gel.

WARRIOR:

1. Using a fairly large brush, paint all the yellow shapes.

2. Use a brush to paint all the pink shapes.

3. Now paint all the green shapes.

4. Then paint all the white shapes.

5. Use a thin brush to fill in all the black details on the color.

6. Finish by painting the rest of the face in black, using a large brush.

CUDDLY CAT:

1. Apply a pink base over the whole face, using a damp sponge.

2. Use a brush to paint in the brown eyes.

3. Outline the eyes in black, using a brush.

4. Use a thin brush to paint in the feathery designs in white, brown, and pink.

5. Use a brush to paint on the black nose, the lips, and the whiskers.

PRETTY POLLY:

1. Using a damp sponge, apply a silver base, and blend over some light blue or lilac.

2. With a sponge, blend orange around the edge of the face.

3. Using a brush, paint in lilac and pink around the eyes, and add pink eyebrows.

4. Using a brush, paint the mouth yellow.

5. Using a fine brush, outline the eyes and mouth in black, and paint in the black nose and mouth. Highlight the eyes in white.

6. Now, using fine brushstrokes, paint lots of different-colored "feathers" all around the edge of the face.

On darker skins some base colors will lose their density. In this case, apply the color in layers, without wetting the sponge in between.

FAKE FURS:

Here is a good example of two faces that have been painted using almost the same design. Just by changing the base color we have created a pink panther as well as a leopard.

1. Using a damp sponge, apply the base color in either pink or light brown.

2. Using a brush, paint in the black eyes, nose, and mouth.

3. Using a brush, paint in white whiskers and outline the eyes. For the leopard, add pink highlights to the nose and whiskers.

4. Using a thin brush, paint the black whiskers.

5. Decorate with spots as in the picture.

    To create different cats you could paint stripes, zigzags, or even fine brushstrokes for a realistic fur effect.

COTTON CANDY:

1. Using a damp sponge, apply a pink base.

2. Using a small brush, fill in the blue eyes and blue lips.

3. Using a larger brush, paint in the lilac shape across the face.

4. Using a thin brush, outline the eyes and the lilac shape in white, and add flashes of pink and lilac to the other cheek.

5. Decorate with glitter gel.

HARLEQUIN:

1. Using a brush, paint in the blue mask.

2. Outline the mask in black, using a brush.

3. Using a fine brush and white paint, mark out guidelines for the crisscross pattern.

4. Using a brush, fill in the shapes you've created with different colors.

5. Outline the diamond shapes in black paint, using a thin brush.

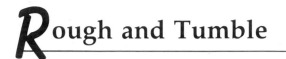

BATFACE:

1. Using a damp sponge, apply a blue base.

2. Blend a little white paint over the lower part of the forehead with a sponge.

3. Using a large brush, outline the bat shape and fill in with black paint.

4. Using a thin brush, paint in black lips, black birds, and a yellow moon.

5. Using a thin brush, highlight the bat with white and paint in the bat's eyes.

6. Use a thin brush to paint in red under the model's eyes. Ask your model to look up as you do this.

PUNK: ▷

1. Using a damp sponge, apply a yellow base.

2. Using a brush, paint the eyes and across the nose in fluorescent green.

3. Using a brush, paint in fluorescent red around the eyes and down one side of the cheek.

4. Using dark blue, paint the rest of the mask and the lips.

5. Use a brush to paint on the ear and neck studs.

The Mohawk wig was bought from a party store. The sides were stuck down with water-soluble spirit gum, and the design was painted up over the bald parts of the wig.

ROBOT: ◁

1. Apply a silver base with a damp sponge.

2. Paint in the black eye-mask, using a brush.

3. Use a thin brush to paint the black lines.

4. Decorate with colored dots and glitter gel, and paint the lips blue.

5. Color the hair green, using water-based makeup.

3 BODY PAINTING AND MOTIFS

You can decorate a body with any pattern you can think of—stars, stripes, wiggly lines, large geometric shapes—it all depends on what you want to do. Body painting can be particularly useful for school plays or dance programs, where a costume would be too difficult to make or would inhibit movement. You can even continue the design over close-fitting fabrics. Always remember to allow yourself plenty of time, and make sure the makeup room is warm enough.

EXOTIC ANIMALS:

The three figures in the photograph below are a good example of the dramatic effects that can be achieved using fairly simple designs.

Base Color

Always apply this with a sponge. Cover every part of the body that shows, including the feet and underneath the arms and hands. Hair color can also be applied with a sponge.

The Design

Using a brush, paint the features on the face first. On the body, outline large areas of color with a thin brush, then fill in with a thicker brush. Use a fine brush to add more intricate details. For a stage production, use bold patterns that will show up from a distance.

Remove the paint in a good warm shower or bath, using plenty of soap.

PUCK:

1. Apply a light green base with a damp sponge.

2. Sponge the sides of the hair in dark green.

3. Using red, yellow, green, and gold, paint the feathery designs over the face and body (we also painted the green leggings).

4. Using a fine brush, carefully paint in red under the eyes.

Beautiful Bodies

The designs shown here are easier and quicker than a full body paint—but are just as much fun.

SUMMER FUN:

The bikini top was first outlined in white and then filled in. The yellow dots were painted on, and then the red lace ruffle. Finally, the top, straps, ruffle, and dots were outlined in black.

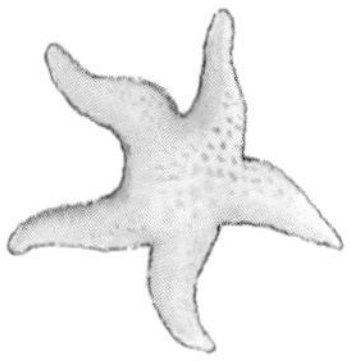

UNICORN:

Sponge the back and arms in blue. Then go over the central area in white for a misty sky effect. Use a thin brush to outline the unicorn head in white and fill in with pink. Add yellow highlights. Paint the horn and mane white. Go over the white areas again if necessary. Outline the head and horn in black. Paint on black eyes, nostrils, neck, and details on the mane.

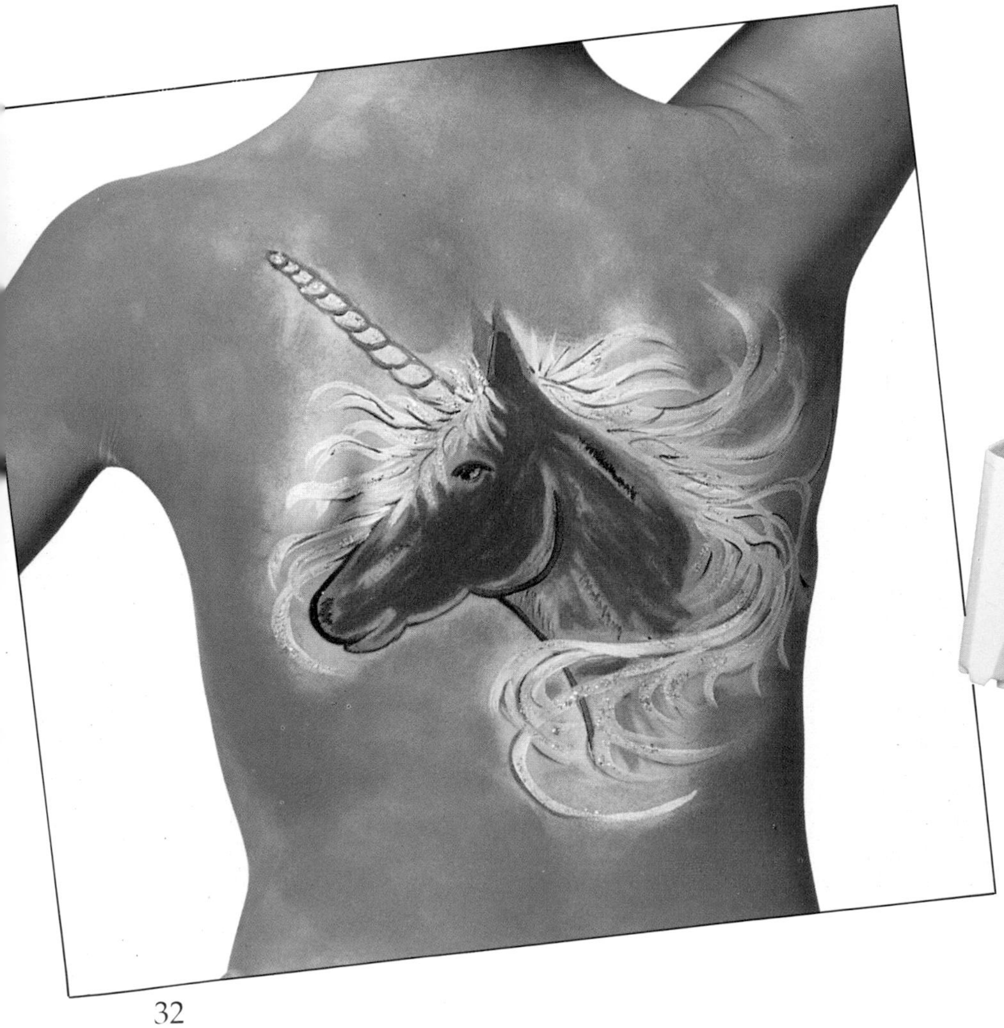

Left: white clouds and blue sky were sponged over the chest. Next, light brown sand was sponged on. The sand castle was painted on in dark brown and the battlements in black. The sun and other details were added last.

ON THE WALL:

Sponge a light blue sky over the chest, and then use a sponge to blend in some white on top to create a misty sky effect. Sponge on an orange or brown base for the brick wall. Paint in the white face shape and hands with a large brush. Outline the face in black, and paint on eyes and the hair curl. Outline the hands in black, and paint the brick outlines in dark brown. Finally, paint the red nose and mouth.

Magic Motifs

Motifs are little pictures or doodles. Not just for the face, but for other parts of the body too. Small motifs can be done almost instantly, making them a great hit at children's parties and outings. The crocodile shown below, for example, would be great fun for a visit to the zoo, or for a team emblem at a football game.

Seasonal or theme motifs are easy to do. For Christmas, paint snowmen, holly, stars, and Christmas trees. For Easter, how about rabbits, chickens, Easter eggs, and spring flowers? On Valentine's Day you could paint roses, hearts, and Cupid with his bow. For Halloween the list is endless.

Carry a little sketch pad around with you so you can copy anything you might see. Ask your friends for ideas, too, and let them try painting motifs themselves. Most people love to paint their feet, and designs such as ballet shoes and sandals look great with costumes.

Ballet shoe

Crocodile

Just for fun, try some motif special effects such as bruises, black eyes, scrapes, and scars—children love to fool adults into thinking they are the real thing. For a black eye, use a barely damp sponge to rub black paint over the eye. Add some red, yellow, and purple for a realistic bruise. Use a stipple sponge with red and black paint mixed together to make a scrape or a scratch. For a scar, paint a thin red line and add small red dots on either side.

Belly dancer's sandal

Fruit above knee

Wrists and finger

Christmas elf

Snowman

4 PUTTING YOUR SKILLS TO WORK

Once you have learned to paint your first few faces, it won't be long before your talents will be required locally. Face painters now appear at fairs, school bazaars, and children's parties, whether it's for profit, fund raising, or just for fun. Water-based makeup has its uses in other areas too. Many schools and drama clubs are finding it easy to use for their own productions. In this section we have concentrated on makeup and simple special effects for theatrical purposes.

Characters and Costumes

One common mistake is to leave the makeup and costumes until the last moment. As soon as you know that your school is rehearsing a play, offer your services. Find out what the characters are and how many will be appearing. Get together with parents and helpers and find out what they can contribute in the way of costumes—either old clothes or materials. Start hunting in thrift shops and garage sales, and even in your own closet.

Begin designing the makeup for the characters as early as you can. Be aware of the time allowed between scenes for costume and makeup changes. Ask the teachers if you can practice the makeup on the main characters before the dress rehearsal, and then make a list of all the makeup materials you will need. Dress rehearsals are always held a day or two before the performance, and you won't have time to change any designs then.

Extras

If you are also dressing the characters, make sure you have plenty of safety pins, needles and thread, scissors, and tape handy.

If you are doing their hair you will need a couple of hairbrushes and combs, along with rubber bands, bobby pins, hair spray, and gel.

The desperado shown opposite is an example of what can be done with good use of face makeup. The aging effect shown here is explained on the following pages.

36

Everybody wants to know how it is done in the movies. On these pages we have included just a few examples of special-effects materials and techniques that you can try for yourself.

A number of special-effects materials are now available—some are suitable for use on children and some are not. Beware of cheap products on the market. Talk to a theatrical supplier and get their advice on whether the product is suitable for your use.

Looking Older

It is very easy to paint faces, but if you want to be able to create more realistic characters you will need to use aging techniques. These are the first techniques that are taught in makeup schools and they include a knowledge of bone structure, shading, and highlighting. It is not as difficult as it sounds, and it will certainly help you to make some faces, such as witches, demons, and old people, look much more authentic.

One good exercise to do is to look in the mirror and study your own face. Feel the sunken areas of your face: for example, the eye sockets, the sides of the forehead, and the hollows of your cheeks. Now feel the places where the bones are more prominent, such as your forehead, your nose, your cheekbones, and your chin. The sunken areas are the ones you shade, and the more prominent areas are the ones you highlight.

As we grow older, lines appear on our faces. Ask your model to screw up his or her face to show you where to paint in lines. Practice doing this on your own face a few times.

For an aging effect, use a barely damp sponge to cover the entire face with a light gray base. Using a sponge, blend in shaded areas such as eye sockets, the sides of the forehead, and the hollows of the cheeks with dark gray. Then use a thin brush to paint dark gray aging lines. Highlight the more prominent areas, such as cheeks, forehead, and nose, using a little white paint on a dry finger. Use a brush to paint over the eyebrows in white, and to apply a little red paint underneath the eyes and add lines to the lips. Lightly use a stipple sponge to create red veins on the cheeks.

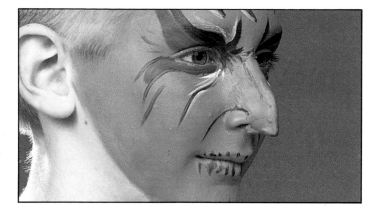

Modeling Wax

Modeling wax (also called dermawax) can be used to change the shape of a face. It is a solid wax and needs to be softened. It adheres to the skin and will stay flexible.

1. Use a plastic spatula or a specially designed modeling wax tool to scrape out some wax from its tub. Do not use too much to start with; it is best to build up the shape you want in layers. Roll the piece of wax between your fingers until it is soft enough to shape.

2. Mold the wax around the part of the face you wish to change—here we have shaped and lengthened a nose.

3. Once you are happy with the shape, paint it to blend in with the surrounding face color. To remove the modeling wax, scrape it off with your fingers and then apply a little cleansing cream. Remove the sticky residue from your fingers with some cold cream.

Crepe Hair

Crepe hair is sold in braided lengths and comes in various colors. It is glued to the skin with water-soluble spirit gum. To make a beard:

1. Cut off some hair to the required length and gently pull the fibers apart. Prepare enough for four or five layers about 2 or 3 inches wide.

2. Apply the spirit gum to the chin, making sure you also cover underneath the chin. Start the first layer of hair underneath the chin. Gently press one end of the fibers against the chin. Don't stick too much of it flat to the skin.

3. Apply the next layer as before, moving toward the front of the chin. Continue until you have enough to create the look you want. You can trim the ends or leave it straggly. To remove, simply pull the beard away and wash the gum off with water.

Water-based makeup is now widely used in dance schools. The vibrant colors, as well as the range of fluorescent and metallic shades, make them very popular with dancers.

Ballet Makeup

On the ballerinas shown here we used a foundation consisting of a cake makeup. This also washes off with soap and water and is available in many different skin tones. It can be applied with a sponge in the same way as water-based makeup.

The eyes should always look dramatic; here we used water-based makeup in a rich blue color to match the dancers' costumes, and outlined the eyes in black. The eyebrows can be blocked out underneath the color by using a very thin layer of modeling wax or special liquid plastic, obtainable from theatrical suppliers.

We used a bright-colored lipstick on the lips, as water-based colors would not be permanent enough to last for a full performance and might smudge as the dancers perspire under the stage lights.

Here are a few ideas for popular characters that often appear in amateur productions.

MARY AND JOSEPH:

On both we applied a base in light brown paint. We added a few aging lines to Joseph's face and darkened his eyebrows by painting over them in black and brown. We used some white on Mary's eyes, and a little ordinary blush makeup on her cheeks. On her lips we used a natural pink lipstick.

THE THREE KINGS:

First King—Use a dark brown base; don't forget the hands and feet. Paint in black eyebrows, mustache, and small beard.
Second King—Apply a light brown base and paint in black eyebrows and a small beard.
Third King—Apply a light brown base. Outline the eyes. Apply a crepe hair beard.

For costumes we used the same basic tunic pattern for all the characters, except for the Third King. For this character we used an old silky blouse, a pair of old pajama pants, and some glittery fabric.

ANGEL:

To make up the angel we sponged on a white base and decorated the eyes with gold paint and glitter gel—being careful not to take the gel too close to the eyes. On her cheeks and lips we used an ordinary pink blush and pink lipstick.

For the costume we used a basic tunic pattern to make the dress. The wings were cut from a piece of cardboard and covered with foil paper. A gold cord was threaded through the center of the wings, crossed over the front of the dress, and tied around the waist. The halo was made from two circles of garden wire, covered with tinsel and yellow ribbon.

FAIRY:

For the makeup, we sponged on a white base and blended in some pink around the outside of the face. We decorated the eyes by painting in pink and lilac, and used a pink lipstick on the lips.

For the costume we decorated a white leotard with sequins (these can be sewn or glued on) and made a circular skirt by gathering several layers of net onto elastic and tying it around the waist. The skirt has sequins on it too.

The fairy tiara, wand, and wings we bought from a party store, but you could make your own by cutting out the shapes from cardboard and painting or covering them with foil paper.

TRAMP:

Apply a light brown base. Use a stipple sponge to dab black paint over the chin for a stubble effect. Paint in black eyebrows, and use tooth black from a theatrical supplier to black out a few front teeth. Use white paint on a sponge to make the hair gray. Use black paint to darken fingernails.

For the costume we found an old suit and washed it to make it go out of shape, then sewed on bright-colored patches. We were lucky enough to find an old top hat, but any old hat would do. Add a bright scarf and an old shirt.

CLOWN:

A traditional pantomime makeup was used here. Apply a white base. Paint in blue eyes, red cheeks, and cupid bow lips. Use a thin brush to paint the eyebrows and eyelashes.

For the costume we used an adult's summer dress and added a red ruffle around the bottom. The waistband and panniers were made from red lining material.

To make the waistband, first measure your model's waist. Cut two wide lengths of the material to fit, allowing a little extra to join them at the back. Sew the two pieces together on the wrong side and turn inside out. Cut two large squares of fabric for the panniers. Hem one side of each and gather the other sides using a long running stitch. Attach the hemmed edge of the panniers to the waistband, leaving a space in the middle. Decorate the waistband with ribbon and attach it at the back with Velcro.

LITTLE DEMONS:

Monster faces can be painted with a variety of colors and designs. The green demon shown here works well on most children. Red luminous face paint can be used around the eyes to make them glow in the dark! The red demon is an easy face to do. A black painted beard or a mustache can also be added.

Halloween is the best time for dressing up. Here are some suggestions for a few popular Halloween characters.

SKULL:

Use a sponge to apply a white base. Blend in a little light green paint over the mouth with a sponge. Paint in the black eyes and nose with a brush. Using a thin brush, paint the eyebrows, the crack across the forehead, and the teeth.

For the costume, make a long black cape with a hood from a dyed sheet. As an alternative, you could use white water-based makeup to paint a white skeleton shape on a long-sleeved black T-shirt and leggings, and cover the hair with a close-fitting hood made from a piece cut from a pair of thick black stockings.

44

WITCH: ▷

Using a sponge, apply a light blue base. Paint in purple eyes and lips. Outline eyes with a thin black line. Use tooth black to black out a few of the teeth. Halloween motifs can be painted on the cheeks. Try painting bats, spider webs, cauldrons, moons, and stars. For the costume, the hat and wig shown here were bought from a party store, although you could make your own hat from cardboard. The skirt, top, and cape were made from black dress fabric.

HAG:

Using a sponge, apply a light green base. Use a brush to paint in dark green eyes, the frown lines, the hollows of the cheeks, and the areas around the mouth. Use a thin brush to paint black outlines around the eyes, cheeks, and mouth. White paint can be added to highlight the center of the nose, the cheekbones, the brow, and the chin. Paint a thin line of red under the eyes. Ask your model to look up as you do this.

45

Because it is so easy to use, water-based makeup is an ideal way of introducing children to the world of theatrical design. Children can be encouraged to design makeup for their own school play, and face painting can be used as an activity at school as part of art or drama lessons.

Getting Things Going

If you decide to run a workshop, we suggest you limit it to children who are at least seven years old. Make sure everyone has an old shirt or apron to wear. Don't make each session too long—an hour should be plenty.

It is essential to show your students the basic techniques first. Begin by demonstrating a whole face. You will find that they won't get bored, but don't choose anything too time-consuming or complicated.

Stress that the makeup sponge should not be too wet when applying the base color, otherwise you will spend the lesson mopping up streaky faces. Show the correct way to apply makeup with a brush: by stroking the brush on the face with firm strokes, not scrubbing with it. Then get them started on their own.

Divide your students into pairs so they can paint each other, but try not to let them all start at the same time. Start each pair off by guiding them on the colors they want to use for the type of face they want to do. While they are waiting, the rest of the group could be working out their designs. At the end, let them go home with their faces painted.

Once the children are familiar with the basic skills, involve them in some project work. They could write a play and design the faces for it.